WO___R

CAROL HARRIS

In Britain, the First World War started in a blaze of volunteering based on patriotism. Millions of people supported the call to defend Britain and its Empire. Many women went to the War Office ready to organise hospital and medical services but, initially, most of these offers were swiftly rejected.

At that time, women had few rights in the home or at work. Many jobs, trades and professions were only open to men; their role was to earn money to support their wives and families, and people believed that 'a woman's place is in the home'. Extending the vote to women was a major political issue and those active in that campaign soon played leading roles in the war – some in support of the conflict, others who actively campaigned for an end to war as a means of settling international disputes.

As the First World War progressed and more men were conscripted, women were needed to carry out work which had previously been 'a man's job'. Government propaganda emphasised that everyone should be doing his or her part – though there was concern at the perceived moral danger posed by men and women working together, and morality patrols were set up to prevent contact between young women and soldiers. Women working in 'new' jobs, such as postal workers, window cleaners and fire fighters, became a common sight on the streets of Britain. And jobs that saw women in more traditional roles, such as nurses, brought women's war work to the fore.

Inequality was ingrained in British society. People were judged by their social connections, class, ethnicity and gender. Women's services in wartime were thus usually led and run by people who were related or 'well connected', and who ran charities in peacetime. But women from all backgrounds found themselves involved in war work in one way or another, from munitionettes to the military.

Women workers were tolerated 'for the duration', while the war lasted, and the First World War couldn't have been won without them. Yet while 1918 saw reform to women's suffrage, historians today still argue about the extent to which the work of women during the war led to permanent change.

Front cover: An American woman assembling gas masks, 1918.

Opposite: Women doing laundry – even mundane tasks were shown to be patriotic.

WOMEN AND THE CALL TO ACTION

*F*rom the beginning of the First World War, women volunteered to support the war effort but the government was reluctant to take up their offers, not least because many who came forward were well known as leaders of the campaign for women's rights.

At this time, women in the United Kingdom could neither vote in general elections nor stand for Parliament, and 'Votes for Women' (women's suffrage) was the major domestic political issue. The campaign had already split into the suffragettes, who used violent tactics, and the suffragists, who rejected violence. The members of the Women's Social and Political Union (WSPU), led by Emmeline Pankhurst and her daughter Christabel, were suffragettes. However, as soon as war was declared the WSPU said it would suspend its campaign of violence to achieve votes for women and instead organise support for the war, a cause it took up with equal vigour.

Patriotic fervour was nurtured in the press and by the government. Women such as those in the WSPU gave white feathers to men not in uniform, in an effort to shame them into joining up by marking them as cowards. The WSPU magazine, *The Suffragette*, changed its name to *Britannia* in April 1915, expelled members who spoke against the war (including Adela and Sylvia, two of Emmeline Pankhurst's daughters) and called for the government to be purged of those who the magazine said were pro-German or 'of German blood'.

With over 53,000 members and 500 branches in 1914, the National Union of Women's Suffrage Societies (NUWSS) was a much bigger organisation. Led by Millicent Fawcett, the society continued the campaign for women's rights by legal methods.

Although women could not vote, many were involved in politics. Working-class women were active in the Women's Co-operative Guild, formed in 1883. Many of its members were pacifists and from socialist, liberal and non-conformist Christian backgrounds. By the outbreak of the First World War, it had 32,000 members and had already campaigned with some success

▲ *The day of the woman worker: Princess Arthur of Connaught opens the British women-workers' exhibition, at Knightsbridge, May 1916.*

◄ *Millicent Garrett Fawcett, leader of the National Union of Women's Suffrage Societies, was from a family of feminist thinkers. Her sister, Elizabeth Garrett Anderson, was the first woman to qualify as a physician and surgeon in Britain.*

WOMEN MUST WORK

One month after the war broke out, Mrs Pankhurst called for 'War Service For All' – compulsory military service (conscription) for men and compulsory war work for women.

In July 1915, helped by a government grant of £2,000, she organised a demonstration of over 30,000 women calling on the government to let women do more to support the war. Their banners proclaimed:

'Mobilise the brains and energy of women'
'We demand the right to serve'
'For men must fight and women must work'

David Lloyd George, the Munitions Minister, supported them, saying, 'Without women, victory will tarry'.

In 1917, Emmeline and Christabel Pankhurst founded the Women's Party. Its manifesto called for drastic measures to support the war effort, and equality at work and in the home for women.

➤ *Factories were often lacking even the most basic facilities. The Young Women's Christian Association appealed for funds to provide accommodation and canteens for women workers.*

for maternity benefits, infant welfare and for a minimum wage, under the leadership of its general secretary, Margaret Llewellyn Davies.

Other women's pacifist movements, from political and church roots, also gathered support as the war went on. In April 1915, British women from the guild and other groups took part in the International Women's Congress for Peace and Freedom, held in Paris. Over 1,100 women attended to protest against the war and to look at ways of organising to prevent future conflicts.

The following year, despite major battles and enormous loss of life on all sides, there was no sign of an end to the conflict known as the Great War. In Britain, support for the war, by now informed by experience, was less enthusiastically patriotic. Compulsory military service was introduced for men aged 18–41 as fewer men volunteered to fight. Women were now needed to work in increasing numbers on the Home Front and to support military forces at home and overseas, and the nature of the call to action for women noticeably changed.

LIFE ON THE HOME FRONT

The First World War was the first conflict in which British civilians were targeted on home soil. Coastal areas were shelled by the German navy and Zeppelin airships dropped bombs on cities and towns – more than 1,400 people died in air raids on Britain. In December 1914, 119 people were killed when the east coast towns of Scarborough, Whitby and Hartlepool were attacked. Public outrage was directed at the German navy for attacking civilians and at the Royal Navy for not preventing it. The ruined homes where women and children had died were shown on posters and postcards.

The government controlled civilian life through regulations passed throughout the war under the 1914 Defence of the Realm Act (DORA). Many women were better off and more independent as a result of their wartime work but shortages, especially of food, led to high prices. There was also widespread poverty and child health was a particular concern. Health visitors and infant welfare services were introduced. Organisations like the Babies for the Empire Society, which campaigned for better infant care and trained children's nurses, said it was a mother's duty to be healthy, so she could produce sons to defend the Empire.

In 1918, Marie Stopes' controversial book *Married Love*, in which she argued for equality in marriage, was published. She followed it, equally controversially, with a book on birth control, though few women were able to plan childbearing.

▲ *Women's influence in encouraging men to volunteer was a common theme, as this 1915 recruiting poster shows.*

GROWING UP POOR

In 1915, the Co-operative Women's Guild published *Maternity*, a collection of letters in which working-class women talked anonymously about the harsh lives they led. One wrote:

When my fourth was born, we had no food or anything to eat, until my husband went to a storekeeper and told him how we were placed, and he trusted us and said we ought to have asked him before. And we all had dinner of oatmeal gruel and tinned milk. The past struggle left its mark on my children. One has died of heart disease aged ten; another of phthisis, sixteen years; my youngest has swollen glands and not at all robust, though not born in poverty, aged fifteen years. I have not been the worst placed woman by a long way, my husband generally having 30s a week [regarded as a good wage], but I could not afford help.

Yes, little one, a Mouse can make dress goods go up quicker than the war.

➤ *Prices at home rose as a result of shortages of essentials such as textiles.*

The British Government's Wartime Propaganda Bureau used images of women extensively in patriotic settings for recruitment campaigns. Often they were shown in posters as victims of a barbarous enemy. Belgium, a neutral country, was invaded by Germany at the start of the war. This was popularly described in Britain as the 'Rape of Belgium' and the country was depicted as a young, female victim. Lurid and usually fictional details of, especially, the treatment of Belgian women and children by the invaders were widely distributed. More generally in posters, women were depicted at home and with children, the message being that the men of Britain had to fight to save their women and country from the same fate.

As time went by, women themselves became the target of recruitment campaigns encouraging them to volunteer for war work. Women working in these new roles became a familiar sight across the country – working on the land, on public transport, in factories and supporting military forces.

Both books were bestsellers despite being banned and condemned for their radical ideas and frankness about sex.

Female morality was likewise of public concern throughout the war; the general view was that soldiers needed to be protected from temptation by 'loose women'. Those whose husbands were away at the front received a 'Separation Allowance' for their children if they had no other income – provided they remained faithful – while DORA regulations were brought in to punish women for spreading sexually transmitted diseases to men. In towns near to army camps, local women organised patrols to deter 'immorality' between soldiers and townswomen.

➤ *Official posters fuelled public outrage at German attacks on British civilians, and at the German invasion on the neutral country of Belgium.*

MEN OF BRITAIN! WILL YOU STAND THIS?

N° 2 Wykeham Street, SCARBOROUGH, after the German bombardment on Dec. 16th. It was the Home of a Working Man. Four People were killed in this House including the Wife, aged 58, and Two Children, the youngest aged 5.

78 Women & Children were killed and 228 Women & Children were wounded by the German Raiders

ENLIST NOW

BELGIAN ✚ RED CROSS

DONATIONS MAY BE SENT TO THE HON. TREASURER, THE RHT. HON. THE LORD MAYOR OF LONDON, OR TO THE PRESIDENT, BARON C. GOFFINET, 28, GROSVENOR GARDENS, S.W.

COPIES OF THIS POSTER MAY BE OBTAINED PRICE 1° EACH FROM 28, GROSVENOR GARDENS, S.W.

SHORTAGES

In 1914, two-thirds of the food eaten in Britain was imported. As a small country with a large empire, Britain had grown dependent on imports of raw materials and food from its colonies around the world. This made the country very vulnerable during wartime, as an enemy could sink the ships bringing those imports, and starve the people into submission.

German U-boats (submarines) began attacking merchant shipping a few months after the start of the war. The U-boat campaign was highly effective and food prices rose dramatically. People attacked and looted shops belonging to those with German-sounding names.

There were soon shortages of food and other essentials in Britain, with widespread accusations of profiteering – making money from the high prices charged for the food and materials that were in short supply. Women were addressed directly in posters and films with advice on how to economise.

By the end of 1916, the shortages of basic foodstuffs such as meat had become a major problem. The Ministry of Food was created and food exports were prohibited. Rationing was discussed – this could ensure food was distributed fairly and not priced beyond the means of all but

▲ *Comic postcard commenting on food queues. 'There's a long long trail awinding' was a popular wartime song.*

FRUGAL FASHIONS

The clothes worn by well-to-do women just before the war had been elaborate and used a lot of material and decorative trimmings. These fashions were a target of the National War Savings Committee. In 1916, it issued an appeal against continuing extravagance in women's dress:

New clothes should only be bought when absolutely necessary, and these should be durable and suitable for all occasions. Luxurious forms, for example hats, boots, shoes, stockings, gloves and veils, should be avoided.

It is essential not only that money should be saved but that labour employed in the clothing trade should be set free.

◄ *1916 poster from the National War Savings Committee.*

▲ 'Waste not, want not' in war economy: women in the hay reserve depot at Richmond shaking out flour sacks in 1916.

the wealthy. The government was reluctant to introduce it, however, fearing public reaction.

Eventually, in July 1917, a national scheme began with the introduction of sugar rationing. Shortly after, it was extended in London and the Home Counties, the most densely populated parts of the country, and 10 million people were issued with ration cards for meat and fats. Bread was another staple food that was in short supply – so much so that King George V issued a proclamation that everyone should cut their consumption of bread by one-quarter. This was particularly difficult for poorer families as bread was a major part of their diet. Bread became more and more expensive until the autumn of 1917, when the government intervened, subsidising the price to consumers so it remained affordable.

Other essentials were unaffordable by this time, and not just imports. There was a shortage of coal – the main fuel for many homes and industries – because there were too few miners to dig for it. Other home-grown staples such

as potatoes and wheat were affected too because there were not enough farmworkers to bring in the harvests. Women had worked on the land from the start of the war but now a recruitment drive was needed to encourage many more to volunteer. The result was the Women's Land Army (WLA), formed in 1917. The following year the government encouraged local authorities to set up National Kitchens and Restaurants. These were to provide properly cooked, wholesome food at cost, using food, fuel and labour effectively. Women who volunteered to run them described their work as 'canteening'.

Rationing proved an effective means of distributing limited supplies of food and so the scheme was extended in 1918. Ration books were simplified and jam was soon added to the list, which also included butcher's meat, bacon, fats and sugar. The scheme continued after the war: meat was rationed until the end of 1919 and the scheme finally ended in 1920.

◀ London ration sheet, 1918.

WOMEN'S LAND ARMY

Women volunteered for agricultural work from the outbreak of the war, but by 1917, food shortages had reached critical levels. The country needed to grow more food at home because enemy attacks on Merchant Navy ships created shortages of imports. Women were thus also needed on the land so that more male agricultural workers could be called up. Farmers were not always keen to employ women and people generally regarded the work as low status, but a national recruitment campaign encouraged them to volunteer. Many of them were workers from munitions factories who were prepared to take a pay cut for a job in a healthier environment.

The Women's Land Army was founded 1917 in response to the shortages. It was organised by Meriel Talbot, who in 1916 had been appointed the first woman inspector for the Ministry of Agriculture. Land Girls, as they were known, were given six weeks' training on specially selected farms to prepare them for working in the fields, milking and caring for animals. A few did specialised work as carters, tractor drivers, thatchers, shepherds or in market gardening.

▲ *Government poster calling for women to volunteer for farm work. With little machinery to help, farming was very hard, labour-intensive work.*

➤ *'Sunshine on the Land' an idealized National Service woman worker from a birthday card.*

◀ *Land Girls at work on a farm.*

SITUATION WANTED

B. A. Ziman spent much of the war working on the land, first in the Women's National Land Service Corps and then in the Women's Land Army. She wrote to the Hon. Mrs Duberley at Eaymes Hall, St Neots, enquiring about work:

I have heard through Mrs Hibbs of Oxfordshire that you are requiring two women for farm work. I have had seventeen weeks of experience on Lord Hood's estate at Barton Seagrave. I left there as soon as the harvest was gathered in, and am now looking for a post over the winter, for a friend and myself. I have done general farm work including haymaking and harvesting and have looked after horses, pigs, bullocks, chickens and have had over a month on dairy work, including the milking of cows. I can give excellent references. Will you please let me know what wages you are prepared to give?

When Women WORK on the Land.

▲ *A humorous view of public concern at the risks of sending unchaperoned young women to work on the land.*

Land Girls joined for six months or a year at a time and the pay was lower than for most other jobs. In 1917, they were paid 18 shillings a week, which increased to £1 a week when they had passed efficiency tests. Farming was labour intensive: there was little mechanisation so the work was physically very difficult. Hardest of all was work in the Women's Timber Service, whose members carried out forestry work.

The WLA uniform, which was issued on loan, included boots, gaiters, clogs, overalls, breeches, hat, jersey and mackintosh, all in brown. Land Girls also wore special armbands with red chevrons to show how long they had served, and lapel badges. Land Girls often wore trousers as the most practical garment for working. They either lived on the farms where they worked, in WLA hostels, or were given billets (lodgings) in the area. Bicycles were also loaned to members. As in other areas of work, the range of jobs done by the women expanded through necessity.

Nationally, the organisation produced a monthly magazine, *The Landswoman*, for members.

It also encouraged local links between the WLA and other groups such as the Girls' Friendly Societies and the Young Women's Christian Association (YWCA). A scheme of Landworkers' Libraries collected donations of books to lend to WLA members.

The Women's Land Army was still needed after the war as food shortages continued, and it was not disbanded until late 1919. By that time, more than 260,000 women had worked on the land during the First World War, 23,000 of them in the Women's Land Army.

Meriel Talbot wrote in the last issue of *The Landswoman* that the WLA had given the opportunity 'for the door [to] open to women to take their place in the agricultural life of the country'. However, as in other areas of work, the change was temporary and only a handful of Land Girls stayed on in farming jobs.

CHARITY AND FUNDRAISING

Charity was a major force in the First World War. Between 1916 and 1920, over 11,000 new charities were registered – an increase of 30 per cent from 1913. Most of these were related to wartime activities, but even donations to non-war charities increased significantly.

Women supporting 'flag days' became a familiar sight on urban streets. Glasgow was the first city in the UK to raise money for wartime charities in this way, collecting £50,000 across 12 days in the first few months of the war. Belgium was an early national cause and donations of clothing and other essentials were gathered to help refugees fleeing the country following its invasion by Germany in 1914.

Wartime charities provided everything a soldier might need. Often, this also meant cigarettes and tobacco. In 1916, the year during which Lady Gertrude Denman chaired the Smokes for Wounded Soldiers and Sailors Society, this single organisation distributed over 265 million cigarettes and other smoking items. Equally popular were 'comforts', such as knitted gloves and socks. Volunteers also made uniforms and other items essential to the war: in schools, girls of all ages (and sometimes boys) sewed rifle covers and sandbags.

The British Royal Family took a far more active role in charities than previously, lending their names as patrons and becoming familiar sights at fundraising events. The Queen Mary's Needlework Guild (QMNG) was one of the best known: established in 1914, it made and

▲ *Postmen call to collect parcels donated for prisoners of war in May 1916. Millions of parcels providing an extraordinary range of items were collected and packed for allied and British troops. Popular items were cigarettes, sweets, Christmas gifts and gloves.*

◄ *Women give up their Easter holiday to pack steel helmets to be sent to troops at the Front, 1916.*

◄ *Queen Mary's needlework and bandage day: gifts being carried into the headquarters in Marylebone, 1916.*

► *Flag sellers were a frequent sight on the streets and might receive a commemorative certificate like this. After the war, servicemen disabled by the war often had to look to charities for help. The National Federation of Discharged and Demobilised Sailors and Soldiers supported.*

distributed clothing and other items to servicemen and to hospitals. It was initially controversial as the work of the guild's volunteers threatened to make unemployment among women in the textile and clothing trades worse. Protests from working women's organisations, trade unions and the Labour Party followed. One result was the Queen's Work for Women Fund, which raised money to give work or help to unemployed women. By the end of the war, QMNG had 630 branches with over 1 million members, not including those in North America.

The Women's Institute (WI), which is today the largest voluntary organisation for women in the UK, was founded in 1915 to meet a specific wartime need. Based on an idea from Canada, its aim initially was to encourage women in rural communities to learn about producing more food from the land.

Although there were many national and well-known organisations, many more were small and local. Charitable work was part of women's lives, across all classes. The parish church continued to be the centre of voluntary action in many areas, although that work increasingly focussed on helping to meet the demands of the war. There was also more demand at home for the support

charities could provide for poorer families. Food kitchens where people could eat cheaply or for free became commonplace as food became increasingly expensive. Charities for men disabled by the war also flourished and collections continued long after the fighting had ended: in 1919, over £400,000 was raised for war charities through 287 street collections in London alone.

APPEAL FOR BELGIAN REFUGEES

When the first appeal came for the Belgian refugees I spoke to the women after church one evening, showed them the pictures of the burnt farms and the poor wanderers, and told them that clothes were wanted for those who had reached England. In a week I had 119 good garments sent to me, old and new, taken out of their own stock – warm long coats, good dresses. One poor farm lad sent two of his own shirts. Since then I have sent a parcel to some fund every month. They buy a tin of cocoa, or milk, or Oxo, or 1lb of rice, etc, and leave it at the vicarage after market; they knit socks, mufflers, mitts, send sheets, pillow-cases, and I send them away. To the Belgian Army we sent 52lbs of provisions, mufflers, mitts, and socks, and 11s in money. That was one month's giving. We have had collections for the National Relief Fund, £4 7s; Local Relief Fund £18; Princess Mary's Fund, £1 2s; and made £11 14s for the Red Cross Fund by a real 'barn dance.'

MARION DEARDEN, A VICAR'S WIFE IN LONG SLEDDALE

PUTTING WOMEN TO WORK

*B*efore the First World War, women's work opportunities were limited. Women often had to give up their jobs when they got married. People believed a husband should earn enough to support his wife, and women should not expect to take jobs that men needed. Most who were employed were in roles regarded as distinctly suitable for women, for instance domestic service, teaching and nursing, and in specific industries such as clothing.

War inevitably created more demand for nurses and hundreds of thousands of nurses and auxiliaries made up one of the largest groups of women working during the conflict. Yet when war broke out, many working-class women became unemployed as their traditional work was cut. It soon became clear that women would be needed in large numbers, however, in work and jobs that were previously open only to men. Even so, employment of women in these areas was slow to begin with.

The introduction of compulsory military service for men in 1916 spurred another jump in demand for women workers. They were employed in an increasing variety of jobs, such as factories and offices, on buses, trams and railways, and as clerks, window cleaners, farm workers and ticket collectors. Women were usually paid a lower rate than men in most jobs. There were a few exceptions – weavers, for example.

▲ *Window cleaners in Cambridge. Women working as window cleaners, chimney sweeps and road sweepers, roles which had usually been available only to men, became a familiar sight in the First World War.*

◀ *Volunteer firefighters were essential when Zeppelin airships started attacking towns and cities on Britain.*

Over 80,000 women were employed by the armed forces in the Women's Army Auxiliary Corps (WAAC), the Women's Royal Naval Service (WRNS) and the Women's Royal Air Force (WRAF). They supported the military at home and in combat areas. Initially employed for domestic and clerical work, women were not involved in the fighting or sent to the front line.

AN ESTABLISHED UNION

The National Union of Women Workers (NUWW) of Great Britain and Ireland was founded in 1895, for 'The encouragement of sympathy of thought and purpose among the women of Great Britain and Ireland; the promotion of their social, civil and religious welfare; the gathering and distribution of serviceable information; the federation of women's organisations and the formation of local councils and Union of Workers'.

At the start of the war it more than 7,000 members and known today as the national Council of Women of Great Britain, it is the oldest surviving women's organisation in the United Kingdom.

The NUWW was concerned with women workers, paid or voluntary and so brought together women from all classes. In 1915, its four-day annual conference covered a wide range of subjects including 'Long hours versus efficiency', 'How the branches meet a new emergency', 'Criminal assaults on children', and 'Medical work among Women in India'.

It main theme was 'Women's Share in the Work of Reconstruction after the War', and members discussed what would be needed postwar in education, industry, legislation and in public health.

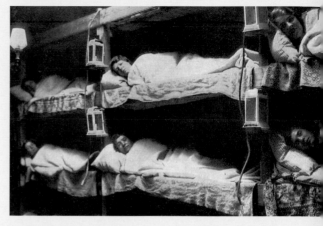

▲ *Few homes had telephones so on-call work often meant sleeping at the workplace, in case you were needed.*

Over the four-year course of the war, 1.6 million women joined the UK workforce. The largest employer was the Ministry of Munitions with 950,000 women workers. Women also joined trade unions, forming women-only organisations such as the Union of Women Teachers, to protect them at work and to campaign for equality in pay and access to jobs.

At the end of the war, women were expected to return to the home. Most were not allowed – and many did not want – to carry on working in 'men's jobs'. One exception to this general rule was the Civil Service, which employed over 100,000 by women by 1921.

Soon, however, they were needed near to where the fighting was taking place, doing dangerous work such as driving ambulances and tending to the wounded while under fire.

Royal Naval, Military & Air Force Tournament
DISPLAY OF PHYSICAL TRAINING BY WOMENS SERVICE

◄ *Events such as this display of physical fitness by volunteers in the Women's Service were good for morale, and showed the public that women were fit enough to take part in war work.*

MUNITIONS AND FACTORY WORK

Factory work in specific industries, such as textiles and clothing, was a common source of employment for women before the outbreak of war. But many lost their jobs as soon as war was declared, because cotton cloth and garments could no longer be exported to markets overseas.

As men were sent to fight, women were employed to replace them and in an increasing variety of trades in factories. Soon they took over most areas of work previously reserved for men in the engineering, chemical and electrical industries.

In 1916, shortages of war weapons began to affect the progress of the war, so the government took over munitions factories to maximise production. Women soon dominated the workforce, but were paid half the wages of men. Employers got round wartime regulations on equal pay by 'dilution' – dividing the work of one skilled man into several less-skilled, lower-paid jobs.

Munitions workers came from a wide variety of backgrounds, attracted by the relatively good pay and independence. They were popular with the public and appeared often in the press.

Many women munitions workers played football to keep fit and most factories had teams. The best known and most successful was Dick, Kerr Ladies from Preston, Lancashire. On Christmas Day in 1917, 10,000 people came to see them play and the match raised £600 – equivalent to £38,000 today – for wounded soldiers.

▶ *The practical demands of war work meant that suddenly women were seen wearing trousers – fashion icons in their own right.*

▼ *Extensive training courses were introduced. These women are at the Shoreditch Technical Institute in London were learning to operate heavy machinery.*

NERVOUS ?
NOT IN THESE TROUSERS !

FRED. SPURGIN

MATERNITY RIGHTS

Pregnant women would often conceal the fact as it would mean losing their jobs. In 1917, medical officer Rhoda Adamson and the superintendent at the National Ordnance Factories in Leeds, H. Palmer-Jones, introduced antenatal care for pregnant munitions workers. Women were given regular health checks, a half-pint of milk and two-course meal daily, and lighter work. A crèche was established so that mothers could return to work earlier with their babies.

'The early notification of pregnancy is entirely a new phenomenon since the workers have come to know that their condition will not now lead to the loss of their own employment', they reported, but the scheme was not taken up elsewhere.

▲ *Stacking shells could be extremely dangerous work. Typically, the women here are wearing no safety clothing.*

▲ *A group of young munitions workers, with careful arrangement of the artillery they have produced.*

The substances they worked with were poisonous, though, and safety measures were primitive with little protective clothing provided. Munitions workers wore distinctive khaki overalls and peg-top trousers, as 'protection' against the corrosive explosive powder. In her book about her time as a 'Munitionette', Joan Williams wrote, 'Women working in larger munitions factories were known as Canaries because they dealt with TNT, which caused their skin to turn yellow. Around 400 women died from over-exposure to TNT during the First World War. Other hazards were more obvious and minor problems were common.'

By 1917, women carried out 80 per cent of all machine work on shells, fuses and trench warfare supplies. They were now building engines and operating heavy machinery such as overhead cranes and lorries. The work was dangerous: casualties in minor accidents were a frequent occurrence, and there were also major incidents. The worst was in 1917, when an explosion at Silvertown in east London killed and injured 73 people and destroyed or badly damaged 900 homes. Women began leaving the industry – relatively well-paid jobs could now be found doing safer work.

In response, the Ministry of Munitions created a Health and Welfare section to boost production and stop workers from leaving for better conditions elsewhere. Laws were passed forcing factories to supply protective clothing, seats in workrooms, washing facilities, drinking water and cloakrooms. The government even produced a film, *A Day in the Life of a Munitions Worker*, which presented an ideal working environment and emphasised the safety measures in the work. Compliance was irregular, however.

As the war ended, women's employment in munitions was cut quickly. By the end of 1918, 750,000 women working in the industry had lost their jobs.

For the general public, among the most visible changes to daily life brought about by the war was the sight of women working on buses, trams and delivering post. Work on public transport was especially popular with women who had previously worked in domestic service. At first, however, there was fierce opposition from employers and trade unions alike across the UK to women doing jobs on public transport, which were previously open only to men.

In 1915, when the Salford Corporation first employed women on its tramways, men refused to work alongside. But by the end of the year, more than half of Manchester's tram conductors were women. As more and more men went into the armed forces, change was inevitable. Trade unions agreed to women filling jobs in transport services, provided they received pay equal to that of men. In fact, many women were still paid less, often as a result of practices such as bonus schemes designed to keep their wages down. Industrial action in public transport was common

▲ *A khaki bus conductress in her new and becoming uniform.*

▼ *'The women workers of the present and future': a mechanic repairing a motor car.*

MRS LLOYD, RAILWAY PORTER

In April 1915, one of the two female porters at Marylebone railway station in London was interviewed by the *Daily Mirror*:

Yesterday the Daily Mirror *found Mrs Lloyd waiting with a group of male porters for the arrival of a train. When the train streamed in she took her place in line with the men, and briskly opened one of the carriage doors.*

Wearing a stout apron over the dress and a man's cap, Mrs Lloyd looked as strong as any of the men.

'I don't mind doing the work at all,' she said. 'My husband is a soldier, and I am doing this to help things along at home.

'I work from eight in morning until six at night, and my wages are 18s. a week, not including any tips I may get from the passengers.

'Tips I have received range from 6d. to 1d. – and I am not too proud to take the money.'

▲ *Female conductors on public transport were known as 'clippies' because they collected and clipped passengers' tickets to show the fare had been paid.*

and thousands of women would go on strike to try to achieve equal pay.

By the end of the war, more than 117,000 women were employed in the transport industries. Some continued to work on public transport after the war and jobs as conductors were open to men and women. Glasgow trained the first women tram drivers.

There was still no possibility of women driving trains but they were employed in railway engineering, varnishing and painting engines. In the railways' workshops, the numbers of women employed went from 43 in 1914 to 2,547 in 1918. Many thousands more became familiar sights as station staff, cleaners and porters.

Women took on heavy work in the dockyards, too, as labourers and in engineering. A 1916 report, 'Labour Finance and the War', listed the range of jobs undertaken by women in the yards:

Attending plate-rolling and joggling machines. Back-handing angle-irons. Flanging. Fitting, uphol-stering, and polishing. Drillers' and caulkers' assis-tants. Plumbers' assistants. Platers' helpers. Rivet heaters. Holders-on. Crane driving. Catch girls. Firing plate furnace. General labouring (gathering scrap and cleaning up vessels in construction).

The Post Office cut back on many of its services at the start of the First World War, but government, business and personal communications were mainly carried out by post, so the volume of mail increased dramatically between 1914 and 1918. Nearly one-quarter of the pre-war Post Office workforce joined the armed forces, so the institution was forced to bring in temporary workers; in the first two years of the war, it employed 35,000 women. For the first time, a full uniform for women was introduced, consisting of a blue serge skirt, coat and blue straw hat. The rule that women had to leave their jobs in the Post Office on marriage was suspended. Typical jobs were in clerical work, as telegraph messengers and delivering mail.

The Post Office distributed official communications such as recruitment forms and ration books. It also assisted the War Office in recruiting thousands of bilingual women who worked on postal and telegraphic censorship, and monitored correspondence with neutral countries.

▲ *A railway version of the popular joke about women working in unexpected roles.*

NURSING ABROAD

◄ British nurses
accompanying the
retreating Serbian army,
January 1916.

▼ Carrying timber for
camp building: a British
Red Cross nurse at
Salonika, January 1916.

*I*t was often argued that women would be too
weak to withstand the sights of war, but this
concern was ignored when extra nurses were
needed to treat those mutilated and gassed by new,
efficient war weapons. Machine guns cut down
infantry in their thousands; gas blinded men and
filled their lungs; wounds were often contaminated
with mud; and life-threatening infections such as
tetanus and 'gas gangrene' were common. Soon
trained nursing staff were taking over doctors' work,
such as triage, inserting drips, giving intravenous
injections and dispensing drugs.

There were many different nursing organisations.
The British Red Cross and St John's Ambulance
amalgamated temporarily, and the Red Cross
nurse became one of the earliest images of women's
service in the war. Voluntary Aid Detachments
(VADs) were the most numerous. Most of them
were women drawn from the upper and middle
classes who had never worked before. They
were not fully trained nurses but were to take
on routine nursing tasks and do whatever else
was needed. In 1915, the War Office agreed that
military hospitals at home and general hospitals
abroad could take VADs, so some also worked as
drivers, clerks and dispensers.

More than 90,000 women served as VADs
during the First World War; 10,000 worked in
hospitals under the direction of the War Office.
Of those, 8,000 served overseas, in France, Malta,
Serbia, Salonika, Egypt and Mesopotamia.

The navy and army had their own nursing
services: Queen Alexandra's Royal Naval Nursing
Service and Queen Alexandra's Imperial Military
Nursing Service respectively. A regular part of
their work was on ambulance trains, which
carried hundreds of wounded men from the
battlefront to hospitals.

THE TWO MADONNAS

Mairi Chisholm and Elsie Knocker set up a dressing station and rest centre for soldiers a hundred yards behind the front line in Pervyse, near Ypres in France. They carried injured men on their backs from the battle and were given the Military Medal for saving a German pilot in no-man's-land – the area between the two sides' forward-most trenches, where either side might shoot at you.

Mairi Chisholm said later, 'We had, funnily enough, over the entrance to the dug-out a little shrine thing, and that's what the soldiers called us – the two Madonnas of Pervyse, and they felt if they fell into our hands, they had every possible chance.'

The two women ran their station for three and a half years until they were injured in spring 1918, in a mass bombing and gas attack. They returned to Britain and ended the war as members of the Women's Royal Air Force.

▲ *British women going to help refugees in Russia: the women's maternity unit at King's Cross leaving for Petrograd.*

On 10 November 1916, three military nurses, Kate Mahony, Ethel Thompson and Mabel Evans, were awarded the Military Medal for their courage on ambulance train 27, during a bombing raid on Amiens. Their commanding officer, W.M. Darling, wrote:

… the explosions crept nearer, until, for us, the climax was reached when at short intervals 5 bombs fell in our immediate neighbourhood, near enough to send debris over the train. Twice the lamps were blown out; windows were broken on both sides of the train. The nearest bomb tore up the off rail of the line next to us, smashed the windows and rocked the coach so much that the patients on one side were thrown out of their cots. The attack lasted an hour.

The Sisters rose to the occasion from the very beginning. Carrying hand lamps they went about their jobs coolly, collectedly and cheerfully. Their influence in stopping panic and allaying alarm, was I believe, greater than that of the officers – just because they were Sisters – patients and personnel felt they had to play up to the standard set by the Sisters. They had their chance and rose to it magnificently.

Probably the most famous British nurse was Edith Cavell, who ran a school of nursing in Brussels. She was shot for treason by the Germans in 1917 for helping soldiers escape to neutral territory. Her death became the focus for international outrage and propaganda, despite her comment the night before her execution, that 'Patriotism is not enough. I must have no hatred or bitterness towards anyone.'

▲ *Edith Cavell at home with her dogs, October 1915.*

NURSING IN THE UK

Hospital services at home were soon overwhelmed with casualties from the battlefields and demand for nurses at home similarly soared. Warfare had been mechanised to an extraordinary level: machine guns fired directly at lines of advancing infantry and gas that poisoned men in the trenches were both extremely effective weapons. Men hoped for a 'Blighty wound' – one just serious enough for them to be sent home to the UK for treatment and convalescence.

There were already some military hospitals in the UK and these now expanded rapidly, often with camps of temporary buildings in the grounds. Civilian hospitals were also turned over to military use and additional hospitals and convalescent homes were opened in large public buildings and stately homes. Specialist hospitals and units were opened to treat the large numbers of men who had psychiatric illnesses, contracted sexually transmitted diseases or lost limbs as a result of war service.

Pat Beauchamp (later Beauchamp Washington) was a member of the First Aid Nursing Yeomanry,

a small group of volunteer women who initially drove ambulances, and ran hospitals and casualty clearing stations for the Belgian and French forces. Beauchamp was badly injured when a train hit her ambulance and her leg was amputated. Back in Britain, she was operated on and sent

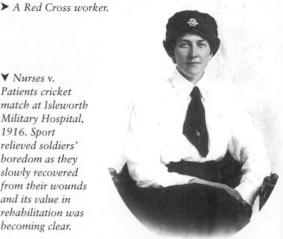

▶ *A Red Cross worker.*

▼ *Nurses v. Patients cricket match at Isleworth Military Hospital, 1916. Sport relieved soldiers' boredom as they slowly recovered from their wounds and its value in rehabilitation was becoming clear.*

Enid Bagnold, later a well-known author, was a VAD when she wrote a memoir, *Dairy without Dates*, published in 1927, while she was nursing at the Royal Herbert Hospital in Woolwich, London. The military authorities had her dismissed from this post because of her criticisms of hospital administration and the attitudes of nurses to their patients. In one extract, she writes:

Sister said of a patient today, 'He was a funny man.'

A funny man is a man who is a dark horse: who is neither friendly nor antagonistic; who is witty; who is preoccupied; who is whimsical or erratic – funny qualities, unsafe qualities. No Sister could like a funny man.

In our ward, there are three sorts of men: 'Nothing Much', 'Nice Boys' and 'Mr Wicks (who has been paralysed).'

Undeterred by the official reaction, Bagnold went to France as a volunteer driver, and published a book about that too.

▲ *Sir John French's Old College at Cambridge, partially turned into a military hospital.*

to convalesce before she could be fitted with an artificial limb, a process which was delayed by bureaucracy and sexism as the system applied only to men. In her autobiography, *Fanny Went to War*, she wrote about visits by strangers – usually well-to-do women involved in charity work – to those injured in battle:

There was a tap on the door. 'Mrs -----', announced the porter and in sailed a lady whom I had never seen before.

I was then put through the usual inquisition, except that if possible, it was little more realistic than usual. 'Did it bleed?' she asked with gusto. I was beginning to enjoy myself. 'Fountains', I replied, 'the ground is still discoloured.'

Civilian nursing in the UK was greatly improved as a result of their wartime work. The College of Nursing was founded in 1916, receiving a Royal Charter a few years later. In 1919, the Nurses' Registration Act set out standards for training, examination and registration, which all those wanting to be nurses had to meet.

Nursing was not the only female profession that became established as a result of wartime service. Almeric Paget's Massage Corps, one of the very few organisations to be recognised early on by the War Office, supplied trained masseuses to work with war wounded in UK hospitals. The corps members also used new treatments such as electrotherapy and hydrotherapy, and developed rehabilitation services for those disabled in the war. Demand for their services increased rapidly. The corps supplied all those giving remedial massage in military hospitals. When the first convalescent camp opened at Eastbourne, 500 of the 3,000 patients were massage cases. Nearly 3,400 people – mainly women – had served in the corps by the end of the war and they went on to help form the modern-day profession of physiotherapy.

▲ *Nurses' fire practice with some rather basic firefighting equipment.*

21

WOMEN'S AUXILIARY ARMY CORPS

*I*n 1916, the War Office concluded that 12,000 British men serving in the army in France in non-combatant roles could be sent to fight immediately, if they were replaced by women volunteers. As a result, the Women's Auxiliary Army Corps (WAAC) was set up in 1917. Mona Chalmers Watson, who was in overall charge, was the sister of Sir Auckland Geddes, who was director of recruiting at the War Office. The corps was headed in France by Helen Gwynne-Vaughan, a recently widowed young woman from an army family.

The two women went to a department store in London and chose a military-style uniform for the WAAC of khaki skirt, jacket and cap. Gwynne-Vaughan was disappointed that women in the corps would be civilians – the army defined them as 'camp followers', the term sometimes used, often pejoratively, to mean anyone who provided services to the military.

Nevertheless, in France Gwynne-Vaughan ran the corps like a military unit. Its members saluted, wore military-style uniforms and used army terms in their work. They were divided into officials (equivalent to army officers), forewomen (sergeants), assistant forewomen

▲ *A 1918 recruiting poster for the new Queen Mary's Army Auxilliary Corps.*

◀ *A formal group of WAACs and army officers.*

(corporals) and workers (privates). WAACs did organised physical exercise every day to improve their fitness.

WAACs took on roles as cooks, waitresses, laundresses, clerks, typists, drivers, printers, gardeners, grooms and tailors. Some technical workers were attached to the Royal Flying Corps (RFC) and others were map-makers with the Ordnance Survey Department. A few experienced linguists replaced British army officers on the General Staff in the Intelligence branch, translating and preparing secret documents.

Gwynne-Vaughan found that, at first, officers and their men objected strongly to the presence of women in military settings. The women were often given the worst facilities, and their work and equipment were sometimes sabotaged. The WAAC soon proved their worth, however. In France, where the corps frequently came under fire from guns and air raids, they suffered casualties alongside the soldiers. The expectation had been that women would never be in such dangerous areas, but they were soon valued for doing essential work, and during the 1918 Spring Offensive, army chiefs argued successfully that it would be difficult to evacuate so many WAACs during a battle.

At this time, a rumour spread, possibly started by German agents, that WAACs were being recruited to France for British army brothels.

▲ *Puns on the initials WAAC were commonplace.*

MARKING A GRAVE

In 1918, six women were wounded and nine died in one of many air raids on Abbeville. QMAAC Marjory Peacock, who knew one of the dead girls, wrote of her funeral:

Graves in France were just long trenches so before Trixie was buried, some of us went out into the woods and gathered daffodils and brought packets of hair pins from the canteen and went down into the grave and lined her part of it by pinning daffodils to the sides before she was buried.

This was so widely believed that in early 1918, the flood of recruits, essential to support the Spring Offensive, almost completely stopped. Eventually, an all-female Government Commission of Inquiry was set up and it concluded: 'The general impression left upon us is of a healthy, cheerful, self-respecting body of young women.' The commission also said that WAACs were less at risk from sexual temptation, and pregnancy among unmarried WAACs was far less likely than was the case for women in civilian life.

Queen Mary frequently demonstrated support for the organisation with official visits, which were covered widely in the press. In April 1918, the Women's Auxiliary Army Corps was renamed Queen Mary's Army Auxiliary Corps (QMAAC).

Over 57,000 women served in the WAAC/QMAAC between January 1917 and 1921, when it was formally disbanded.

WOMEN'S ROYAL NAVAL SERVICE

including the welfare and control of members when off duty.

Vera Laughton Mathews, director of the first training school for WRNS at Crystal Palace in south London, later wrote:

> I cannot honestly say we collected a company of superwomen ... 1918 was the last year of the war, the cream of the girls had gone, were already in war work, and a very large proportion of our Crystal Palace Wrens were only half-fledged, just the minimum age of eighteen.
>
> The recruits reported in batches of twelve to twenty every fortnight and the unit grew to nearly three hundred, one of the biggest in the service. They had two weeks' training before starting their duties, squad drill, PT and lectures about the Navy. At the end of the fortnight they were enrolled ... and when uniform was available they were kitted up.

The Women's Royal Naval Service (WRNS), whose members were known as Wrens, was created in November 1916. Its original purpose was to recruit 3,000 women who could take over the UK-based jobs of Royal Navy men so they could go on active service overseas. The WRNS recruited its volunteers for 'shore service', which meant that they were to stay on land – the WRNS's unofficial motto was 'Never at Sea'.

Originally, the intention was for them to do clerical and domestic work, but soon the need to send more and more men on active service with the Royal Navy meant that the Wrens' range of duties expanded. By the end of the war, Wrens were working in large numbers in wireless telegraphy, as dispatch riders, postwomen, code experts, electricians and engineers. Some actually did take to the water, as boats' crews.

The first head of the organisation was Dame Katherine Furse. She had been commander-in-chief of the Voluntary Aid Detachments but resigned in 1917 because she was prevented from introducing reforms. Immediately, she was offered the post of director of the new service. She was responsible for every aspect of the WRNS,

In the announcement calling for volunteers, published in *The Times* in 1917, recruits were promised 'a distinctive uniform', but Wrens wore civilian clothing until January the following year. When it did arrive, the uniform was immediately a talking point.

The version for officers was rather smarter than officers' uniforms in other services, but the outfit for the Wrens ratings (lower ranks) was less popular. The main garment was a coat-dress in a rough, thick serge. It buttoned up the front to an uncomfortably high neck and was topped and tailed with a pudding basin-style hat with a round brim and pleated crown, and a pair of heavy boots. Insignia were in blue instead of the Royal Navy colour of gold, and stripes denoting rank were topped off in a diamond shape instead of the men's curled pattern. As with the other women's services, some Wrens were needed after the war too, taking on the jobs of serving men who were demobilised. The WRNS was finally disbanded in 1919. At its peak, during WWI, it had over 7,000 members.

▲ *Women munitions workers for the fleet: polishing a vessel's propeller.*

◄ *One branch of munition work done by women and girls: making naval searchlight projectors and signalling lamps.*

WRENS ALL THEIR LIVES

Vera Laughton Mathews wrote about the First World War work of the WRNS in her book, *Blue Tapestry*:

[The WRNS] had a far-reaching effect on many who served in it, probably largely because service of that kind was so new to women ... To feel themselves really useful at a time when the country had its 'back to the wall' ... gave them a new dignity. They went back to ordinary life imbued with the romance of service. I believe that they felt themselves Wrens all their lives.

At the end of the war, Mathews writes, women were given no choice as to whether they stayed in the service: 'They were given one week's pay in lieu of notice; that was all and some of them felt very bitter indeed about it.'

WOMEN'S ROYAL AIR FORCE

For most of the war, the air stations of the Royal Naval Air Service and the Royal Flying Corps were staffed with Wrens and WAACs. In 1918, over 9,000 volunteered to move to the Women's Royal Flying Corps, forming the nucleus of the WRAF service when it was founded on 1 April 1918, the same day as the men's Royal Air Force (RAF).

The first two commandants, Lady Gertrude Crawford and the Hon. Violet Douglas-Pennant, complained about the lack of support as they tried to build the service. The government ordered a report, which was highly critical of Douglas-Pennant, who was dismissed. Helen Gwynne-Vaughan, the Overseas Commander of the Women's Army Auxiliary Corps, replaced her.

At first, wages were based on existing experience and skills, and little training was given. But the military need for more specialised support forced changes, and soon women joined the WRAF in the hope of learning a trade.

▲ Copies of this studio portrait of a WRAF in uniform would be given to friends and family and sent as postcards.

▲ WRAFs gather for a more formal photograph.

➤ *On Armistice Day, 11 November 1918, members of the Women's Royal Air Force wave flags to celebrate the end of the war.*

There were two groups of members: 'Immobiles' lived at home but were attached to a nearby station; 'Mobiles' lived in quarters and could be sent anywhere. Selection was rigorous and involved medicals and other assessments: many women from poorer backgrounds were rejected because they were physically unfit. Typically, WRAF officers were drawn from the middle and upper classes.

The work of the WRAF was divided into four trades: clerks and storewomen, household, technical, and non-technical. Most members were clerical workers. Shorthand typists earned the highest pay; those in the household section the lowest (though they worked the most hours). The technical section was the most highly skilled. The range of WRAF trades included aircraft riggers, armourers, mechanics, electricians, tinsmiths, welders, balloon operators and engineers.

There were particular problems with clothing the new force. At first, the majority, who transferred from the WRNS or WAAC, had to sew the new WRAF badges over their old blue or khaki uniforms. New recruits were supposed to wear new uniforms in RAF blue but supplies were slow to arrive so they often had to wear their own clothes. There were many complaints from members as the working conditions were often wet and dirty. In June 1918, the National Parade of Servicemen was held without WRAF representation because of the shortage of uniforms.

Here, as with the WAACs, the morality of the women in the service was a public concern so standards of behaviour were set out in a lengthy constitution and rulebook. Among the rules was one that specifically forbade WRAFs from smoking in the street, whether on or off duty. Smoking was a new and popular wartime habit.

From March 1919 – four months after the end of the war – thousands of WRAF members were sent to France to take over the jobs of men returning home. More than 300 served in Cologne, Germany, as part of the Air Force of Occupation. By this time they were working in more than 50 trades, from photography to pigeon-keeping. In total, more than 32,000 women served in the WRAF but, after this final burst of activity, it was disbanded on 1 April 1920.

THE LAST SURVIVOR

The last surviving veteran from the First World War was Florence Patterson, who joined the WRAF when she was 17, in September 1918. She spent the next ten months serving meals in the officers' mess at RAF Marham and then at RAF Narborough, both in Norfolk.

In an interview in 2010 she said, 'I met dozens of RAF pilots and would go on dates. I also had the opportunity to go up in one of the planes but I was scared of flying.

'I worked every hour God sent but I had dozens of friends on the base and we had a great deal of fun in our spare time. In many ways, I had the time of my life.'

After demobilisation, she married Walter Green, a railway worker and they lived in King's Lynn, Norfolk. Mrs Green died, aged 110, in February 2012.

WOMEN ABROAD

MRS. WYNNE IN WESTERN TRENCHES   3632-6

▲ *Hilda Wynne, a military officer's widow who drove ambulances and supported relief efforts across Allied territories, was arguably the most decorated woman worker of the First World War. She served on the British, French, Belgian and Russian fronts.*

New organisations such as the military-style Women's Emergency Corps and the Women's Legion were ready to offer medical, nursing and domestic services to help the British military forces, but most offers were swiftly rejected by the British Government.

In 1914 in Paris, the Women's Hospital Corps opened a hospital for the French Red Cross. It was such a success that the British War Office asked the corps to organise a hospital at Womereux, France, attached to the Royal Army Medical Corps (RAMC). It was the first time medical women had been treated equally with male doctors by the British Government. The two doctors who led the corps, Louise Garrett Anderson and Flora Murray, also established a 17-ward military hospital in London run and staffed by women.

Elsie Inglis, a doctor and secretary of the Scottish Suffrage Societies, also offered to equip a hospital for injured soldiers and run it with an entirely female staff. When the British Government refused to support her plan, she pressed ahead independently, raising £200,000 and setting up the Scottish Women's Hospitals for Foreign Services. Members wore distinctive grey uniforms with tartan flashes and thistle decorations, khaki shirts and ties, and Homburg hats. Over the next four years, Inglis organised women's units of doctors and nurses to run hospitals in conflict areas across Europe. When her hospital was overrun by the enemy, she was briefly taken prisoner. Upon being repatriated, she went to another unit in Russia.

Another large organisation was the Women's National Service League, organised by Mabel

WINTER RETREAT

Flora Sandes fought with the Serbian army in the mountains of Macedonia and was decorated and promoted to sergeant major. In her book, *An English Woman-Sergeant in the Serbian Army*, published in 1916, she wrote about the retreat from invading Bulgarian soldiers:

We had one of the slowest, coldest, rides you can imagine. There was a piercing blizzard blowing across the snowy waste, blinding our eyes and filling our ears with snow; our hands were numbed, and our feet so cold we could hardly feel the stirrups. We proceeded in dead silence, no-one feeling disposed to talk, and slowly threaded our way through crowds of soldiers tramping along, with bent heads, as silently as phantoms, the sound of their feet muffled by snow.

St Clair Stobart. She had run similar services in war zones before the First World War broke out, and now took teams of doctors and nurses into Belgium, France and Serbia. Dr Mabel Ramsay was a surgeon in the Women's Imperial Service Hospital at Antwerp. In her diary for 24 September 1914 she wrote of Stobart:

we received fifty patients and thereafter we were rapidly filled up so that we never had a vacant bed and on the night of the bombardment we had 135 cases, some lying on the floor on mattresses ... At 8.30 work began in the hospital and continued more or less all day and night, as very soon wounded came in only during the night, after the battles of the day. Many had been 24 hours without receiving first aid. All work at night could only be done by means of candles or shaded lights, as the whole of Antwerp was shrouded in darkness ... once or twice we had telephone messages from the forts that even this meagre light was too much. This meant, of course, that no serious operation could be done at night, other than dressings, so that operations were deferred unless extremely urgent until daylight ...

In gratitude for our work Mrs. Stobart was presented with two gilt medals of the King and Queen of the Belgians, and we had a pretty ceremony at which the Marseillaise was sung and God Save the King played on a tooth comb by a Belgian soldier.

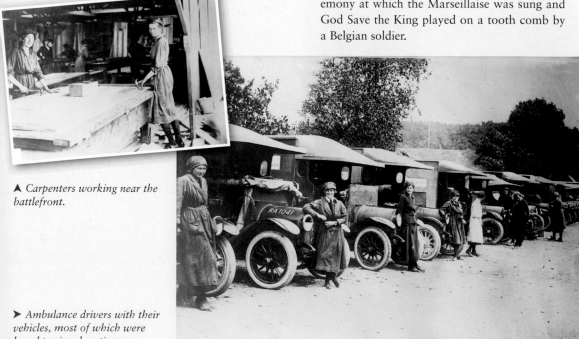

▲ *Carpenters working near the battlefront.*

➤ *Ambulance drivers with their vehicles, most of which were bought using donations.*

The piano or new phonograph were the centre of entertainment in the wartime home. People bought sheet music and records of songs made popular by leading singers to play at home, and patriotic songs about the war became popular. Edna Thornton, a famous classical singer, recorded *Your King and Country Wants You*, which was sung throughout the war.

People went out to the cinema, theatre or the music hall. The raucous atmosphere of the music hall encouraged recruitment. The audience would sing along to patriotic songs performed by popular entertainers, and men would be invited on stage to volunteer for military service before the performance ended.

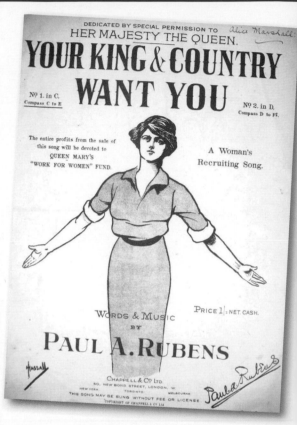

▲ *'A Woman's Recruiting Song', sung by Edna Thornton for HMV in 1914.*

One of the best-known stars – and the highest paid – was the male impersonator Vesta Tilley, who became known as 'Britain's Best Recruiting Sergeant'. Dressed as a soldier, she sang songs such as *Jolly Good Luck to the Girl Who Likes a Sailor*, *Six Days' Leave* and *I'll Make a Man of You*. Another song popular throughout the war was *Keep the Home Fires Burning*, which tells women to be cheerful and brave for the soldiers who 'dream of home'. The lyrics were written by an American, Lena Gilbert Brown Ford. She and her son were the first US citizens to be killed in an air raid in London when their house was hit by a bomb in March 1918.

At this time, films were silent so brief captions were inserted to explain events. People read newspapers and could see something of life in

▲ *Male impersonator, Vesta Tilley, who was known as Britain's best recruiting sergeant because of her patriotic songs.*

the trenches in silent newsreels, especially in the enormously popular propaganda film, *The Battle of the Somme*.

The war also prompted pro- and anti-war poetry. Jessie Pope, a journalist and poet, wrote patriotic poems such as 'The Call' and 'Who's For the Game?', which were published in the *Daily Mail*.

As time went on, the realities of war were increasingly reflected in poems such as Eileen Newton's 'Last Leave':

Let us forget tomorrow! For tonight
At least, with curtains drawn, and driftwood
    piled
On our own hearthstone, we may rest, and see
The firelight flickering on familiar walls …

Official war artists painted for the government propaganda department. One of the first war artists was Anna Airy, who was commissioned to

◄ *Author Vera Brittain as a nurse in 1918.*

do a series in munitions factories. While painting a shell forge on Hackney Marshes, her shoes melted in the intense heat.

Many people kept diaries and published memoirs during and after the war. One of the best known is *Testament of Youth*, by Vera Brittain, in which she wrote of the deaths of her brother, her fiancé Ronald Leighton and her friends in the war. She recorded in her diary visiting Ronald Leighton's mother and sister, who had just received his returned kit:

The garments sent back included the outfit that he had been wearing when he was hit. I wondered, and I wonder still, why it was thought necessary to return such relics – the tunic torn back and front by the bullet, a khaki vest dark and stiff with blood, and a pair of blood-stained breeches slit open at the top by someone obviously in a violent hurry.

PEACE AND AFTERWARDS

*E*dith Summerskill, later a Labour MP, was a medical student in London in 1918 when she wrote about the end of the war:

It was during a physics lecture on the morning of 11 November that a messenger hurriedly entered and whispered to the Professor. A normally shy, reserved man, his face was suddenly wreathed in smiles and he turned to the class and announced, 'An Armistice has been signed. You are dismissed.' We leapt from our seats and yelling with excitement and relief we poured into the Strand. The pent-up agony of the First World War was shared by the whole nation and my generation were especially sensitive to the appalling casualty lists. Young servicemen friends would visit us before leaving for the front and cynically toss a coin to decide whether they would return to see us again.

The feminist Millicent Garrett Fawcett wrote in 1920 that the war had:

revolutionized the industrial position of women. It found them serfs and left them free. It not only opened to them opportunities of

▲ *Celebrating victory in a dress and cap representing the flags of the Allied nations.*

employment in a number of skilled trades, but, more important even than this, it revolutionized men's minds and their conception of the sort of work of which the ordinary everyday woman was capable.

By the time she wrote it, however, most women had returned to the home and the pre-war rules preventing them from working in many trades and professions had been reintroduced. According to the 1921 Census, 25.4 per cent of women in Great Britain were employed, which was the same proportion as 1911.

Some things had changed, however. Greater independence during wartime meant that many women aimed for factory work as an alternative to domestic service. Women continued to work

▲ *Women military motorists celebrate the signing of the Armistice.*